Medieval Medicine and the Plague

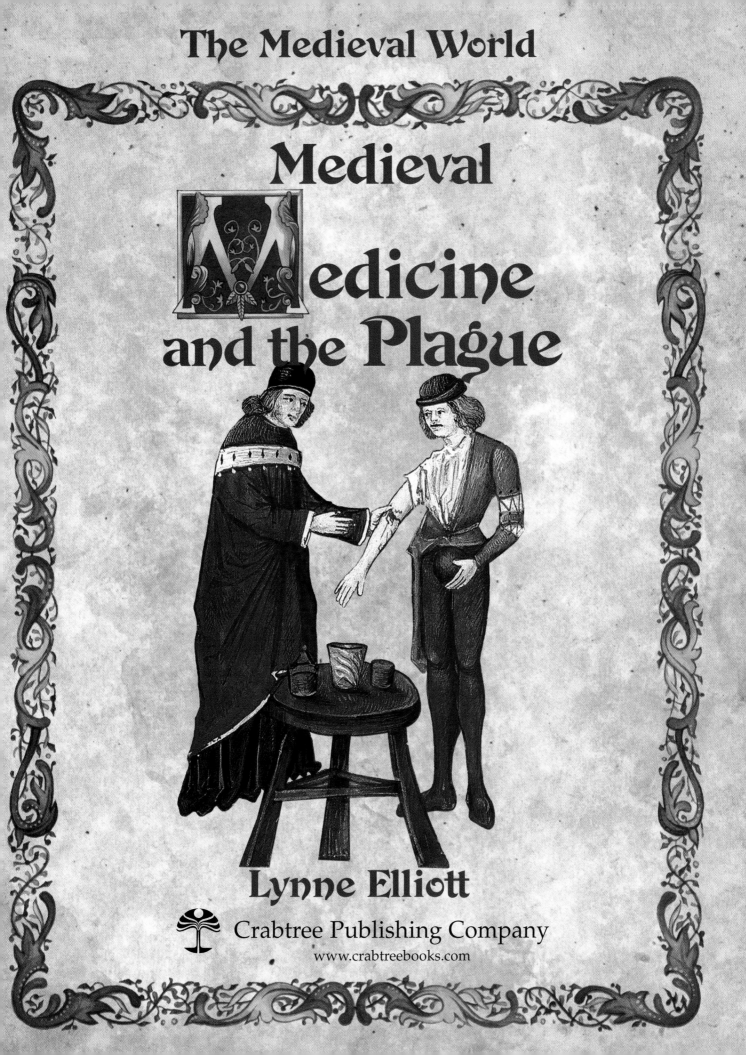

Lynne Elliott

Crabtree Publishing Company

www.crabtreebooks.com

Crabtree Publishing Company

www.crabtreebooks.com

Coordinating editor: Ellen Rodger

Series editor: Carrie Gleason

Designer and production coordinator: Rosie Gowsell

Scanning technician: Arlene Arch-Wilson

Art director: Rob MacGregor

Project development, editing, photo editing, and layout:
First Folio Resource Group, Inc.: Tom Dart, Greg Duhaney, Sarah Gleadow, Debbie Smith

Photo research: Maria DeCambra

Consultant: Isabelle Cochelin, University of Toronto

Photographs: Alinari/Art Resource, NY: p. 6 (left), p. 14 (top), p. 15 (top), p. 17; Art Archive/Biblioteca Augusta Perugia/Dagli Orti: p. 7 (bottom); Art Archive/Biblioteca Nacional Lisbon/Dagli Orti: p. 20 (top); Art Archive/Biblioteca Nazionale Marciana Venice/Dagli Orti: p. 16, p. 18 (left); Art Archive/Bibliothèque Mazarine Paris/Dagli Orti: p. 31; Art Archive/Bibliothèque Universitaire de Médecine, Montpellier/Dagli Orti: p. 22 (top); Art Archive/Cathedral Treasury Aachen/Dagli Orti: p. 26; Art Archive/Musée Condé Chantilly/Dagli Orti: p. 24 (right); Art Archive/Museo Diocesano Orta/Dagli Orti: p. 13 (top); Art Archive/Private Collection/Dagli Orti: p. 25 (bottom); Art Archive/Saint Sebastian Chapel Lanslevillard Savoy/Dagli Orti: p. 9 (left); Art Archive/University Library Prague/Dagli Orti: p. 23 (center); Art Directors/Foto Werbung: p. 15 (bottom); George Bernard/Science Photo Library: p. 7 (top); Bettmann/Corbis: p. 6 (right); Biblioteca Monasterio del Escorial, Madrid/Giraudon/Bridgeman Art Library: p. 30 (right); British Library/Egerton 2572 f.51v: p. 13 (bottom); British Library/HIP/The Image Works: title page; British Library/Royal 6 E. VI f.503v: p. 22 (bottom); British Library/Sloane 1975 f.93: p. 24 (left); British Library/Topham-HIP/The Image Works: p. 23 (top), p. 23 (bottom); D.Y./Art Resource, NY: p. 18 (right); Chris Hellier/Corbis: p. 29; Musée de l'Assistance Publique, Hôpitaux de Paris/Archives Charmet/Bridgeman Art Library: p. 28; Musée Atger, Faculté de Médecine, Montpellier/Lauros/Giraudon/Bridgeman Art Library: p. 25 (top); Musée Condé, Chantilly, France/Giraudon/Bridgeman Art Library: p. 30 (left); Pierpont Morgan Library/Art Resource, NY: cover; Scala/Art Resource, NY: p. 12, p. 19; Snark/Art Resource, NY: p. 5, p. 14 (bottom); p. 20 (bottom), p. 21 (right); Courtesy of the Trustees of Sir John Soane's Museum, London/Bridgeman Art Library: p. 8; C. Walker/Topham/The Image Works: p. 27 (left); © Walters Art Museum, Baltimore/Bridgeman Art Library: p. 9 (right); Wellcome Library, London: p. 21 (left), p. 27 (right)

Map: Samara Parent, Margaret Amy Salter

Illustrations: Jeff Crosby: pp. 10–11; Katherine Kantor: flags, title page (border), copyright page (bottom); Margaret Amy Salter: borders, gold boxes, title page (illuminated letter), copyright page (top), contents page (background), pp. 4–5 (timeline), p. 4 (pyramid), p. 32 (all)

Cover: A doctor examines a dying patient's urine, while family and friends pray for the patient's soul.

Title page: In the Middle Ages, patients visited doctors' offices to be bled and to have their urine examined in order to balance the body's four fluids, or humors.

Crabtree Publishing Company

www.crabtreebooks.com   1-800-387-7650

Cataloging-in-Publication Data
Elliott, Lynne, 1968-
Medieval medicine and the plague / written by Lynne Elliott.
    p. cm. -- (The medieval world)
Includes index.
ISBN-13: 978-0-7787-1358-6 (rlb)
ISBN-10: 0-7787-1358-X (rlb)
ISBN-13: 978-0-7787-1390-6 (pbk)
ISBN-10: 0-7787-1390-3 (pbk)
1. Medicine, Medieval--Juvenile literature. 2. Black Death--History--Juvenile literature. I. Title. II. Medieval worlds series.
R141.E45 2005
614.5'732--dc22

**Published in
the United States**
PMB 16A
350 Fifth Ave.
Suite 3308
New York, NY
10118

**Published
in Canada**
616 Welland Ave.
St. Catharines
Ontario, Canada
L2M 5V6

**Published in the
United Kingdom**
73 Lime Walk
Headington
Oxford
OX3 7AD
United Kingdom

**Published
in Australia**
386 Mt. Alexander Rd.
Ascot Vale (Melbourne)
VIC 3032

Table of Contents

Medieval Medicine

The Middle Ages, or medieval period, began around 500 A.D. and ended around 1500 A.D. in western Europe. Lords, such as kings and great nobles, ruled most of the land. They granted less important nobles smaller parcels of land, called manors, in return for their advice and military service.

Peasants, who made up 90 percent of the population, lived in villages in the countryside. They worked on the land, growing food and raising animals for their lords and themselves. Other people, including craftspeople, bankers, shopkeepers, lawyers, and doctors, lived in towns and cities.

▶ *In the Middle Ages, kings, great nobles, and well-known knights held most of the power, land, and money. They often had private doctors and received the best medical care available. Peasants usually did not have access to trained doctors and had to cure themselves.*

540
The Plague of Justinian, the first plague to affect a large part of the world, begins

700
Japan's "age of plagues" begins, and Japan suffers more than a hundred separate epidemics of smallpox and measles, which last until 1050

1000
Avicenna, an Iranian scientist, writes *The Canon of Medicine*, one of the most important medical books of the Middle Ages

1080
The medical school at Salerno, Italy, is established

1123
St. Bartholomew's Hospital is founded in London, England

1136
The Pantokrator Hospital is founded in Constantinople, in present-day Turkey

1250
The first anatomy lessons are taught at Salerno's medical school

1315
The first dissection of a human corpse is conducted in Bologna, Italy

▲ *A deadly disease called the Black Death, or Black Plague, came from Asia in 1347. Ships traveling with cargo, diseased people, rats, and fleas spread the disease from southern Europe to the north.*

Health in Cities and the Countryside

During the Middle Ages, people's health depended on where they lived. Fleas and rats spread diseases in both cities and the countryside. Sewage and garbage polluted water supplies, making water unsafe to drink. Fortunately, townspeople who became ill were able to visit nearby doctors, surgeons, and apothecaries, from whom they bought medicines. Peasants, who lived far away, had to make their own medicines when they were sick, set their own bones when they broke, and stitch up their own wounds.

▼ *Contagious diseases spread more quickly in crowded, dirty cities than in the countryside.*

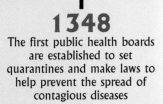

The Black Death begins to ravage southern Europe
1347

1348
The first public health boards are established to set quarantines and make laws to help prevent the spread of contagious diseases

Medieval Diseases

Many kinds of illnesses and diseases affected people throughout the Middle Ages. Some of the most common ailments were bone fractures, head wounds, and burns, caused by accidents and warfare.

Diseases Caused by Poor Hygiene

Skin infections were common among peasants and townspeople. They wore rough wool clothing and lived with lice, fleas, bedbugs, and other insects that irritated the skin. People bathed only once a week or less because of the effort it took to fill bathtubs. Most places had no running water, so water had to be carried from nearby wells or rivers and heated before being poured into a tub.

▶ *Often, broken bones that healed poorly had to be broken again by surgeons and set in splints so they would heal straight.*

▲ *Stomach viruses and food poisonings sometimes caused people to vomit.*

Diseases Caused by Poor Diets

Poor diets and bad food caused many diseases. A lack of vitamin C, which is found in fresh fruits and vegetables, caused a disease called scurvy. Scurvy loosened teeth and made gums spongy.

Medieval people did not eat a lot of raw fruit and vegetables because they thought they caused stomachaches and diarrhea. In fact, dirty water and foods infected with **bacteria** led to most stomach upsets and to serious diseases such as **dysentery**, typhoid fever, and **cholera**.

Infectious Diseases

Viruses, spread by human-to-human contact, affected many medieval people because there were no medicines or **vaccines** to stop the diseases from spreading. Measles, smallpox, and chicken pox caused high fevers, skin blisters, scarring of the skin, and many deaths. Severe throat and chest infections, such as diphtheria, influenza, and whooping cough, spread quickly and killed many people in a short period of time. These viruses sometimes struck a population and then disappeared, only to return and cause many deaths years later.

▲ *Medieval people, like the nobleman in this photo, suffered from heart attacks and strokes.*

Leprosy

Leprosy was a common and frightening disease throughout the Middle Ages. It attacked a person's skin, nerves, eyes, and breathing. People with leprosy lost fingers, limbs, and even the tips of their noses.

People thought leprosy was contagious, so the sick were separated from family and friends, and were sent to live in houses called leproseries. If they traveled outside leproseries, they had to wear distinctive clothing and warn people of their approach by rattling a clapper or bells. Today, even though leprosy is easily treated, people in poorer parts of the world still suffer from the disease because of inadequate medical care and the lack of money to buy medicine.

▶ *It was the duty of religious men and women to care for the sick in the Middle Ages. They set up hospitals and leproseries to care for people with leprosy.*

The Black Death

The Black Death, or Black Plague, was the most terrifying disease of the Middle Ages. It struck Europe from 1347 until 1351, killing one in four people.

The Black Death was not the only plague to afflict Europeans in the Middle Ages. They suffered a terrible plague in the 500s A.D., and plagues appeared at different times up to the early 1700s.

The Spread of the Black Death

The Black Death came to Europe on 12 trading ships from central Asia. On the ships, which docked in Italian seaports, were crew members who were dead or gravely ill with the disease. Townspeople sent the ships away, but it was too late. They had become infected with the Plague, and began to spread the disease to one another. The Plague spread northward as infected people traveled from town to town.

Three Types of Plagues

The Black Death was a combination of three types of plagues: bubonic, septicemic, and pneumonic. The bubonic plague was caused when a flea infected with the bacteria *yersinia pestis* bit a human. The flea's bite sent the bacteria into a person's **lymphatic system**. Painful bumps, called buboes, developed in the groin, armpits, or neck. If the bumps broke open and the poisonous bacteria spilled out, a person could survive the disease. If the bumps did not break open, people died less than three days after the first bump appeared.

◄ *Some people believed that God brought plagues to punish them for their sins. While marching in religious processions, they prayed for God's forgiveness and for a quick end to the deadly disease.*

Septicemic and Pneumonic Plagues

Septicemic plague was caused when the deadly bacteria infected a person's bloodstream instead of the lymphatic system. Bacteria in the bloodstream multiplied so quickly that there was no time for symptoms to develop. People who felt fine died within hours.

Pneumonic plague resulted when a person infected with the Plague developed pneumonia and began coughing up blood. Every time a person coughed or talked, bacteria spread onto the person's clothing or into the air. People who touched the sick person's clothing, as well as others nearby who breathed the bacteria-filled air, became infected. Pneumonic plague was the deadliest plague. It killed almost everyone infected within a few days.

▲ *The Black Death struck suddenly. People sometimes developed buboes filled with blood and pus, and got chills, fevers, and headaches. The fever sometimes caused them to convulse, or shake, violently. They were said to be doing "the dance of death," or the* **danse macabre.**

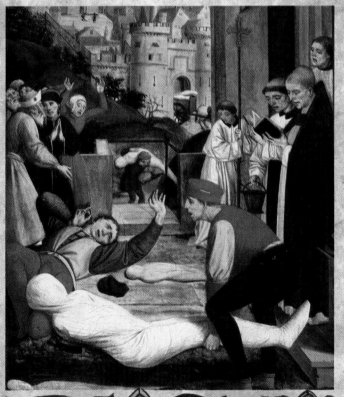

Trying to Stay Healthy

Medieval doctors did not know what caused the Plague, as we do now. They realized, though, that the Plague traveled by air and that it spread when healthy people came into close contact with those who were infected. To avoid the Plague, doctors suggested that townspeople move to the countryside, where there were fewer sick people. They also recommended that healthy people avoid the sick by staying inside and not attending festivals or other public events.

◀ *Many religious men and women became ill and died after taking care of people suffering from the Black Death and burying the dead.*

Plague Horrors

The Black Death affected entire families, towns, and cities at the same time. Family members were often too ill to bury their dead, so many people were not buried at all.

Black flags were flown from church steeples, warning visitors not to enter the infected area.

In cities, the bodies of those who had died were left on doorsteps for workers to pick up in wagons for large, quick burials.

If people had to go outside, doctors recommended that they cover their noses and mouths with apples covered in spices, scented handkerchiefs, or bags of herbs to cleanse the bad air.

Buboes were sometimes as small as almonds or as big as apples.

People with the Black Death sometimes vomited, became dizzy, and spat up blood.

Doctors advised people to close their windows and cover them with thick curtains to keep the "poisonous air" out of their homes.

During the Black Death, some people stole from shops whose owners were sick with the Plague.

Medical Beliefs

People in the Middle Ages were not sure what caused diseases, including the Black Death. Many of their ideas came from their religious beliefs. They believed that God sent illnesses as punishment for people's sins or to test their strength and faith. The cure was to pray to God and give charity to the poor.

Other people's theories, or beliefs, about illnesses were based on scientific ideas of the time. They thought that the movement of the planets caused bad air, which affected people's health and caused diseases.

The Humors

The most important explanation for illness in the Middle Ages came from ancient Greek beliefs about sickness. The ancient Greeks thought that people became ill when there was an imbalance in the body's four fluids, called humors. The four humors were black bile, yellow bile, phlegm, and blood.

To restore the four humors to a proper balance, medieval doctors recommended special diets, exercise, and hot and cold baths. They prescribed purges, or laxatives, which were mixtures of herbs added to food or drink to get rid of too much of one humor. Bloodletting, in which doctors, surgeons, or barbers, cut patients' veins to drain blood, was also believed to help rid the body of excess blood.

▼ *Medieval people visited the tombs of holy people, called saints, to ask for the saints' help in curing family members and friends who were sick.*

Medical Beliefs in Other Cultures

Doctors in medieval India and China had ideas about medicine that were similar to European doctors' theories about the humors. Doctors in medieval India believed that seven parts of the body, including blood, flesh, fat, bone, and marrow, had to stay balanced. According to Chinese doctors, people were healthy when two forces, called yin and yang, were in balance. Like European doctors, Indian and Chinese doctors prescribed herbal medicines to balance the body's elements and help people regain their health.

"Living Seeds of Disease"

Around the 1400s, some scientists began to suspect that diseases were caused by tiny particles that they called "the living seeds of disease." These tiny particles could not be seen by the naked eye. It was only when Dutch scientist Anton van Leeuwenhoek invented the simple microscope in 1674 that people could see bacteria. Then, they realized that diseases were caused and spread by bacteria entering the human body through cuts and scratches in the skin, by breathing air with bacteria in it, and by eating food **contaminated** by bacteria.

▲ *People in the Middle Ages believed that mental illness was caused by an imbalance of humors affecting the brain or by an evil spirit that had taken over a person's mind. One cure was to have a priest exorcise, or get rid of, the demon by praying.*

Humors and Your Personality

The English adjectives for types of personalities come from the Greek and Latin names for the four humors. Choose the personality type that best describes you.

- Black bile (*melagkholikos*): "Melancholic" means sad or gloomy.
- Blood (*sanguineus*): "Sanguine" means cheerful.
- Yellow bile (*khole*): "Choleric" means easily angered.
- Phlegm (*phlegma*): "Phlegmatic" means calm.

▶ *The four humors described personality types and the "four ages of mankind": childhood (top left), when people are melancholic; youth (top right), when people are sanguine; adulthood (bottom left), when people are choleric; and old age (bottom right), when people are phlegmatic.*

Home Remedies

Medieval women made many of their families' medicines at home. They used herbs, trees, and flowers that they grew in their gardens, and animals that they raised. These ingredients were mixed into food and drink, added to bath water, or mixed with animal fat to make skin lotions.

Herbs

People believed that herbs cured everything from headaches to nervousness. Sweet marjoram was thought to purify blood, dill to cure stomachaches, and mint to stop bleeding and heal dog bites. Rue was believed to sharpen eyesight, and mint and anise to cure bad breath. Skin creams made from the sap of fig trees were said to remove warts, and drinks made from the sap of maple trees were thought to cleanse the liver.

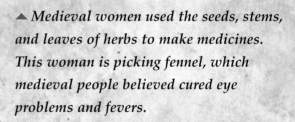

▲ *Medieval women used the seeds, stems, and leaves of herbs to make medicines. This woman is picking fennel, which medieval people believed cured eye problems and fevers.*

◀ *Medieval people cut the trunks of trees to collect juices, called resin or sap, to use in medicines. Balsam resin, which is very fragrant, helped treat dry, cracked skin and cure breathing problems. It was also used in perfumes.*

▲ Medieval women prepared special foods to cure certain illnesses. They believed that eating beets cured dandruff, blisters, sores, and other skin problems. Women in southern Europe served pasta to people with colds because they thought it was good for the chest and throat.

Flowers

Flowers were used to treat many ailments. Medieval people made an ointment from roses, which they rubbed on their temples to cure headaches. A lotion made from daisies healed skin wounds. A drink made from the dried flowers of an herb called chamomile stopped stomach cramps, and a drink made from daffodil bulbs, which are very poisonous, healed upset stomachs by causing people to vomit.

Medicines Made from Animals

Animals and animal products were used in medieval medical recipes. Women dropped warm hens' fat into ears to heal earaches. They mixed salmon oil and bees' honey into an ointment for eye problems. They rubbed pigs' dung on noses to stop nosebleeds, and dabbed geese droppings on cuts to heal the skin.

Herbs from Around the World

Like women in Europe, women in the **Middle East**, India, and China prepared medicines using herbs and spices from their gardens. Women in the Middle East used raw garlic to treat asthma and other lung diseases, as well as toothaches. They mixed coriander into tea to cure stomachaches, and added cumin to food to soothe aching joints. In India, drinks made from berries, dates, grapes, and cinnamon bark healed all kinds of ailments. In China, saffron was used to help sadness, and ginger was used to heal stomachaches.

▶ In the Middle Ages, cinnamon was used to cure stomachaches and improve circulation.

15

The Apothecary

Apothecaries owned shops in towns where they prepared and sold medicines that were too difficult to make at home. They mixed herbs, spices, and animal products to make ointments that were rubbed on the skin, syrups or pills that were swallowed, and lozenges that were sucked on.

Recipe Books

Many medicines at apothecaries' shops were combinations of ingredients found in recipe books of medicines. Books of medicines were often translations of ancient Greek and **Arabic** texts that listed the benefits of hundreds of plants and drugs.

One of the most difficult drugs to mix was theriac, also known as treacle, because it was made from 64 ingredients. Theriac was one of the most famous and expensive drugs in medieval England. People believed it cured everything from pimples to heart problems.

Many of the apothecaries' medicines were extremely expensive because they were made from ingredients that came from far-away places. Ginger, from China, and cinnamon, from Sri Lanka and India, helped improve digestion. Cloves, from the Spice Islands, were believed to ease tooth, gum, and muscle pain. Sugar, from the Middle East, was believed to purify the blood and cure kidney and bladder problems.

▲ *Apothecaries ground herbs for medicines using club-shaped tools called pestles and bowls called mortars. They carefully weighed each ingredient using different sizes of scales.*

Training to Be an Apothecary

Apothecaries learned their skills by working as apprentices, or assistants, to experienced apothecaries called masters. At first, an apprentice's duties included bringing ingredients to the master and keeping the shop and tools clean. Eventually, the apprentice learned to mix medicines on his own.

Many apprentices were trained by apothecaries to treat illnesses. Some apothecaries were very good at diagnosing sickness, and were known as experts in their trade. Others misdiagnosed their customers and caused them harm. They were punished by losing their shops, and they were forbidden from practicing their trade ever again.

More than Medicine

Besides medicine, apothecaries sold salt and spices, such as pepper, sugar, cinnamon, cloves, cumin, and saffron, which medieval people used to flavor their food. They also prepared perfumes, shampoos, soaps, cosmetics, and dyes for clothing from the herbs and spices in their shops.

▼ *An apothecary's shop was filled with bottles, bowls, and large jars that held ingredients for medicines, such as flour, sugar, wax, honey, oils, and lard, or animal fat.*

Doctors

Doctors in the Middle Ages diagnosed illnesses and prescribed treatments. They also advised people on how to prevent diseases from spreading.

Making a diagnosis involved taking the patient's pulse, examining the color, clearness, and smell of a sample of urine, and looking at the patient's other fluids, such as blood and phlegm. Doctors also performed brief physicals, or examinations, of the patient's body and asked about the patient's diet, general health, and physical activity.

For treatment, doctors recommended bloodletting, medicine, changes in diet, or better personal hygiene, such as taking frequent baths and brushing one's teeth. They also prescribed exercise, such as horseback riding, fencing, hunting, or dancing, to noble clients. If a doctor was unable to make a diagnosis, he asked another doctor's opinion or suggested to the family ways to keep the sick person comfortable until he or she died.

Clothing and tools distinguished doctors in the Middle Ages. University-trained physicians often wore long robes. They were often depicted in art as holding a flask, or bottle, of urine, since they examined urine when diagnosing illnesses.

Quarantining

To prevent illnesses from spreading, doctors usually suggested separating, or quarantining, people who were sick from those who were healthy. This was especially important during times of contagious diseases and plagues. Doctors also helped town authorities make laws to improve people's health, such as laws about removing garbage and sewage and keeping water clean.

Doctors' treatments included prescribing tonics, or healthy drinks, that they made themselves or ordered from apothecaries.

Educating Doctors

Medical schools were established in the late 1000s, but very few doctors attended them before the 1200s. Most doctors received their education by watching and working with more experienced doctors. After 1200, when increasing numbers of universities began to teach medicine and grant medical degrees and licenses, more doctors were required to attend medical school.

Only men could go to European universities; women were forbidden from attending. Men in medical schools were usually the sons of nobles or wealthy townspeople who had done well in their first few years of university.

▲ Some doctors made house calls to examine the sick. Other doctors saw patients in their offices or at infirmaries in town hospitals or in monasteries. Still other doctors served as private physicians to kings and other nobles.

Medical School

Medical school lasted seven years, during which students attended lectures by learned physicians and read books about the causes of disease and the medicinal uses of herbs. They also learned about anatomy, which is the study of the human body. Ancient Greek and Middle Eastern physicians wrote these medical books long before the Middle Ages.

Medical students also dissected, or cut apart, animals to learn about anatomy. They did not dissect human bodies since it was considered cruel to treat a body that way. It was not until 1315 that an Italian professor performed the first dissection of a human corpse at the medical school in Bologna.

▲ *Medical students had to see patients with an experienced physician for six to eight months before graduating. These new graduates were called university doctors.*

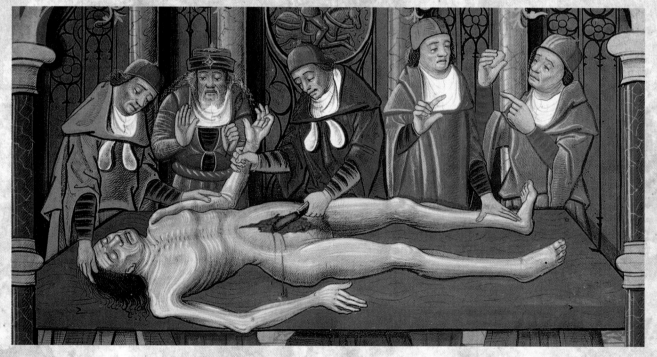

▲ *After doctors began dissecting human corpses, they gained a better understanding of the human body, including the stomach, heart, lungs, and skull.*

Hippocrates

Among the physicians who influenced medieval doctors the most was Hippocrates. Hippocrates was a Greek physician who lived around 400 B.C. He established the rules and principles, called the Hippocratic Oath, that were followed by medieval doctors and are still followed by physicians today. In this oath, doctors promise to take care of the ill and not do them harm.

Galen

Galen was a Greek physician who lived in Rome around 150 A.D. He wrote hundreds of books about topics such as human anatomy, surgery, and herbal medicines. Medieval universities used Galen's works as their main textbooks, but some of his ideas were incorrect since he could not dissect a human body to see what was inside.

Hippocrates is called "the Father of Medicine" because of his writings, especially about the four humors.

◀ Rhazes

Rhazes, also known as Ar-Razi, was born in Iran in 865 A.D. He was the first person to describe the smallpox and measles diseases. He also became an expert in children's illnesses. Rhazes' ten-volume book on medicine and diseases, called *The Book of Medicine*, became an important textbook in European medical schools.

Avicenna

Avicenna, also known as Ibn Sina, was an Iranian physician and scientist who lived from 980 A.D. to 1037 A.D. He wrote one of the most important medical books of the Middle Ages, *The Canon of Medicine*, which deals with diseases, anatomy, and medications.

Surgeons

Surgeons in the Middle Ages fixed broken bones, treated bug bites and bee stings, and bandaged and stitched wounds. They performed bloodlettings, cuppings, and cauterizations, which made up the majority of surgical procedures. They also performed major operations on people who were in extreme pain or in danger of dying.

Most surgeons received their training by working as apprentices to more experienced surgeons. Some also took a few courses in medical school.

▲ *A medieval surgeon uses a sharp knife to operate on a patient's neck while an assistant holds the patient steady.*

Barbers

Medieval barbers, or barber-surgeons, cut hair and shaved men's faces. They also performed minor surgeries, such as removing rotten teeth and bloodletting. The symbol of the barber, the red and white striped barber's pole, comes from the practice of bloodletting. The red stripes represent the blood that was "let," or released, and the white stripes represent the bandages used to cover the cuts. Like most surgeons, barbers did not go to medical school. Instead, they apprenticed with more experienced barbers.

◄ *Barber-surgeons removed their patients' rotten teeth with pliers. They may have placed the teeth on a rope that they wore around their necks.*

Bloodletting

Bloodletting was the most common form of surgery and treatment in the Middle Ages. In bloodletting, surgeons, barber-surgeons, and doctors opened veins with knives to drain out some of the patients' blood. The blood was caught in a bowl and examined for excess humors. Blood was also "let" to release excess humors from the body. Medical textbooks showed which veins to cut to release each humor and to cure different illnesses, such as heart disease, kidney pain, or liver problems. Surgeons also applied leeches, or small bloodsucking worms, to the skin to remove poisons or bad blood from a wound.

Cupping ▶

With cupping, surgeons placed a hot metal glass or cup on a patient's cut skin. They believed that the hot cup drew a gentle flow of blood to that spot so that dangerous poisons would be released from the body. They also thought that heat from the cup would soothe sore muscles and skin injuries. The medieval practice of cupping came from the Middle East, where steam baths, called *hammams*, provided cupping as a service for customers.

◀ Cauterizing

Surgeons sometimes cauterized wounds, which means they burned skin tissue with red-hot irons or boiling oil. They believed that cauterizing helped seal wounds to prevent fatal infections and bleeding to death. They also believed that cauterizing helped heal internal disorders. Textbooks showed surgeons where to place hot irons or oil to cure each ailment.

Operating

Lancing and removing boils, setting broken bones with splints and stiffened bandages, and removing shattered bone fragments were among the operations that medieval surgeons performed. More difficult surgeries included removing tumors, **hernias**, and stones that formed in the kidneys and bladder. These surgeries were usually only done as a last resort because people often died as a result of the operations.

▶ *Medieval surgeons practiced trepanning, where they removed a piece of the skull to release pressure that caused severe headaches.*

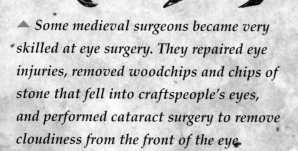

▲ *Some medieval surgeons became very skilled at eye surgery. They repaired eye injuries, removed woodchips and chips of stone that fell into craftspeople's eyes, and performed cataract surgery to remove cloudiness from the front of the eye.*

Medieval Anesthetic

To anesthetize patients, or put them to sleep, surgeons made patients cover their noses and mouths with sponges soaked in extremely strong, and often dangerous, drugs. These drugs included opium, mandrake, and hemlock. Surgeons learned about the drugs from Arabic medical textbooks. Patients also drank dwale, a drink made from hemlock, lettuce, opium, wine, and pig's bile, as an anesthetic. Sometimes, the anesthetic did not work and the patient woke up during surgery. The surgeon kept on operating even though the patient could feel everything and was often in a lot of pain.

Surgical Instruments

Some surgeons in the Middle Ages were trained in the metal trades, and made surgical instruments for themselves and for other surgeons. Surgeons cleaned their instruments before operating using egg whites and wine or other alcohol.

▲ *Brass needles pulled thread made of wool, silk, linen, horsehair, or gold and silver wire through the skin to close up wounds. Some needles were hollow, and were used to suck out fluid during eye surgery.*

▲ *Knives, or scalpels, which pierced and cut into the skin and tissue, were used as drills to break up kidney stones, and were heated in fire and used to cauterize wounds.*

▲ *A bow saw was used to cut through bones. Saws for cutting bones varied according to the size of bone they had to cut through.*

▲ *Round-headed tools were used as probes to explore inside the body.*

▲ *Bone scrapers were used to remove pieces of bone that had decayed, or broken down, because of disease.*

Surgeons in Other Cultures

Hindu doctors in India were experts in doing plastic surgery to repair noses and ears. They also set bones with splints made of tree bark and pieces of bamboo. Arab physicians were skilled at performing eye surgeries to remove cataracts and heal other common eye diseases. They were the first to use animal gut to stitch up wounds, and they developed a plaster used to make casts for broken bones.

◀ *Chinese doctors used acupuncture, or the pricking of the body with needles at different points, to cure diseases and ease pain. Charts such as this one showed where on the body to insert needles in order to heal various types of illnesses.*

Female Doctors

Female doctors were less common than male doctors in the Middle Ages. Females who did practice medicine played an important role, especially in women's health.

Many women, because of modesty, refused to be seen by male doctors and died because they did not seek medical care. As well, male doctors were not allowed to examine some parts of a woman's body, such as her stomach. Female doctors, who also treated male patients, did not have these restrictions.

Midwives

In the Middle Ages, babies were born at home in the mother's bedroom. Midwives helped deliver the babies, as did female relatives and neighbors. Men were not present at the birth.

▼ Many medieval women died giving birth because of infections or because they lost too much blood.

Midwives made the mother comfortable by rubbing ointment on her belly and offering her comforting words throughout the labor. When the baby was born, the midwife cut the umbilical cord, washed the baby with water, and dried it with linen cloths. She wrapped, or swaddled, the baby tightly in linen bands. This kept the baby warm, and some people believed it helped the baby's bones grow correctly. Then, the midwife placed the baby in a cradle next to the mother's bed and made sure the baby was fed and cleaned every few hours.

Three Female Medical Experts

Some medieval women became experts in medicine even though they were not allowed to attend university. They received their medical education by studying on their own or by apprenticing with their husbands or fathers who were doctors, surgeons, or barbers.

◀ Hildegard of Bingen

One of the most learned and respected women of her time was Hildegard of Bingen, a German **nun** who lived from 1098 to 1179. Hildegard wrote books about music, poetry, history, science, and religion. She also wrote a medical book called *Causes and Cures*, which contained details of health disorders and diseases, advice on curing and preventing illnesses, and recipes for herbal medicines.

Trotula ▶

Historians are still debating whether a female doctor named Trotula, who may have practiced medicine in Salerno, Italy, sometime between 1050 and 1250, actually existed. She, or male doctors who used her name, wrote books about general health concerns, such as toothaches and deafness, as well as about women's health, pregnancy, and female beauty and cosmetics.

Jacqueline Félicie de Almania

Jacqueline Félicie de Almania was a doctor who practiced medicine in Paris, France, in the 1320s. She was popular among female patients, who preferred seeing a woman doctor to a male doctor. She made her own medicines and had great success curing sicknesses. This success made male doctors and medical teachers at the University of Paris angry, so they tried to prohibit her from treating patients on the grounds that she did not have a university degree or a license to practice medicine. She was fined and ordered to abandon her medical practice. She ignored the order and continued to treat her patients.

Hospitals

The earliest medieval hospitals, or infirmaries, were set up in monasteries and run by religious men and women called monks and nuns. They cared for the sick, the poor, and others in need. Infirmaries also housed travelers, the homeless, the elderly, and abandoned children.

Large monastery hospitals were built to let in a lot of light and air, which were thought to improve people's health. The main ward, or room, was a large open hall with high ceilings and large windows. The walls were decorated with beautiful murals and paintings. Large hospitals also had a garden in which plants were grown for medicine, storerooms, a bloodletting house, a bathhouse, and a kitchen.

◀ Medieval hospitals were supposed to be clean and quiet, but they were often noisy and crowded places. Beds were lined up in rows, and two or three sick people often shared a bed, so there was no privacy.

Infirmarians and Doctors

The head of the hospital was called an infirmarian. Infirmarians were not trained physicians. They, along with monks and nuns, cared for the sick by bathing them, feeding them, preparing medicines for them, and making sure they were comfortable and clean. Infirmarians also prayed for the sick and dying. Physicians, who either lived at the infirmary or came in from town, diagnosed and treated the patients.

Hospitals in Towns

In addition to monastery hospitals, hospitals were set up in towns near the main church or just outside the town gates. The size of hospitals varied from three to four beds in small town hospitals to 200 beds in large city hospitals. Local governments often ran these hospitals, and they were supported financially by donations from wealthy townspeople.

▶ *The Pantokrator Hospital of Constantinople, in present-day Turkey, was founded in 1136 by Emperor John II as a monastery. It included a leprosery, a retirement home for the elderly, two hospitals, one for men and one for women, a kitchen, a pharmacy, and baths. In addition, it offered medical teaching.*

The Knights of St. John

The Knights of St. John grew out of a group of monks called the Hospitallers. Around 1080, the Hospitallers set up a hospital in Jerusalem, in the **Holy Land**, to care for Christian **pilgrims** visiting the city. The hospital had more than 2,000 beds.

Beginning in the early 1100s, the monks developed into a fighting order of knights to defend against **Muslim** attacks. The Knights of St. John fought in the Holy Land until Muslim victory in 1291. In 1877, members of the British order of St. John established St. John's Ambulance, which today provides emergency care and first aid classes.

▶ *The symbol of the Knights Hospitaller, a white cross with eight points, was visible on the knight's surcoat and shield.*

Death and Burial

In the Middle Ages, most people died at home surrounded by friends, family, and neighbors. People were buried within two or three days of their death.

Preparing for the Funeral

The first day after a person died, female relatives lit candles around the bed of the deceased, washed the body, and tightly wrapped it in a shroud, or sheet, made of a rough material called sackcloth. The very wealthy were dressed in fine burial clothes with jewelry and symbols of their power, such as crowns for kings.

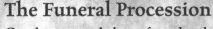

◀ *Wills were prepared so that people who died could leave gifts to family members, friends, and religious organizations. Gifts included shirts, shoes, cooking fuel, firewood, food, and money.*

The Funeral Procession

On the second day after death, family and friends put the body on a wagon for a procession to the church. They rang a bell to let people know that the person had died so that others could pray for him or her. Some people also believed that funeral bells scared away demons that might attack the soul of the dead person. The more important the person, the larger and more impressive the procession.

▶ *A priest performed Last Rites for a person who was dying. He said special prayers and placed holy oil on the person's eyes, ears, lips, nose, hands, feet, and back.*

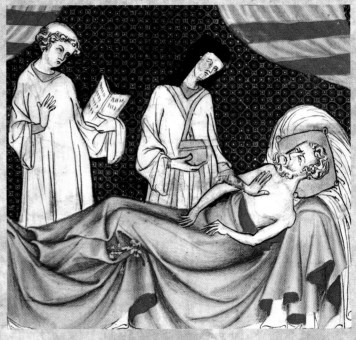

The Funeral

Six pallbearers carried the body into the church. If the person was wealthy, the body was placed in a coffin, but more often it was placed in a reusable box that the church owned. The box was then carried through the church on a cart, or metal rack, called a hearse. The hearse had holders for candles, and it was usually draped with a black cloth. Mourners gathered at the church for a funeral service, during which they said prayers for the dead person.

On the third day, the body was buried in the churchyard, usually just in the sackcloth shroud. Kings and very important nobles were buried in stone coffins in the floors or walls of their family **chapels**, important churches, or monasteries.

After the Funeral

After the funeral, the family of the person who had died prepared a meal for the mourners and priest. The meal often consisted of bread, cheese, wine, or a weak alcoholic drink called ale. At the funeral of important people, servants prepared meals with two or three courses, including lamb, chicken, or beef flavored with expensive spices.

▼ *A hearse holding candles and a coffin stood before the altar until the funeral service was finished.*

Glossary

Arabic The written and spoken language of the Arab people

bacteria Microscopic organisms that sometimes cause disease in plants, animals, or people

chapel A building or room for religious worship

cholera A contagious disease that causes vomiting, cramps, and diarrhea

circulation The movement of blood through the body

contagious Able to spread from one person to another

contaminate To make impure or unclean

dysentery A disease of the bowel that causes stomach pain, fever, and severe diarrhea

hernia A condition in which one of the body's organs pushes out on the wall that contains it, causing a bulge

Holy Land An area in present-day Israel, Jordan, and Syria that has special religious meaning for Christians, Muslims, and people of other religions

knight A medieval soldier who fought on horseback, mainly with swords

lymphatic system The system that protects the body against infection by destroying bacteria

Middle East The region made up of southwestern Asia and northern Africa

monastery A community where monks or nuns live, work, and pray

Muslim Belonging to the religion of Islam. Muslims believe in one God, called Allah, and follow the teachings of his prophets, the last of whom was Muhammad

nun A female member of a religious community who devotes her life to prayer and study

pilgrim A person who makes a religious journey to a holy place

priest A person who leads religious ceremonies in the Catholic Church

vaccine An injection that protects a person against a specific disease

Index

1 2 3 4 5 6 7 8 9 0   Printed in the U.S.A.   4 3 2 1 0 9 8 7 6 5